Ice Babies in Oz

L.E. McCullough, Ph.D., was born on Bastille Day in Speedway, Indiana, the year Troy Ruttman won the Indy 500.

He's worked as a book publisher, college teacher, radio announcer, film and videomaker, concert promoter, entertainment publicist, journalist, record producer, arts administrator, advertising copywriter and musician, recording with numerous Irish, French, Cajun, Latin, blues, jazz, country, bluegrass and rock ensembles on 30 albums for Log Cabin, Kicking Mule, Rounder, Bluezette and other independent labels. He is the author of *The Complete Irish Tinwhistle Tutor* and *Favorite Irish Session Tunes*, two highly acclaimed music instruction books, and has composed filmscores for three PBS specials—*Alone Together, A Place Just Right* and *John Kane*. His poems and short stories have been published in 88 North American literary journals, and he has received 33 awards in 24 national literary competitions. His play, *Blues for Miss Buttercup*, is co–winner of the 1994 Mill Mountain Theatre New Play Competition and is set for Off Broadway performance in 1995 by Playwrights Preview Productions of New York.

Formerly Assistant Director of the Indiana University School of Music at Indianapolis, Dr. McCullough is currently employed as Executive Director of the Palenville Interarts Colony in Palenville, New York. Dr. McCullough is a member of The Dramatists Guild, Inc.

Ice Babies in Oz

Original Character Monologues For Actors

by L.E. McCullough

Monologue Audition Series

SK
A Smith and Kraus Book

A Smith and Kraus Book
One Main Street PO Box 127 Lyme, NH 03768

First Edition: March 1995
10 9 8 7 6 5 4 3 2 1

Library of Congress Cataloging-in-Publication Data

Acknowledgments

The author wishes to thank the following for professional assistance in theatrical development:

Frances Hill, Maggie Cahill, Patricia Floyd, David Shepherd and T.L. Reilly of Playwrights Preview Productions, Linda Charbonneau of the Indiana Theatre Association, Audrey Cunningham of University of Indianapolis, Clare Marshall McClure of Indiana University–Purdue University at Indianapolis, Judith Baumel of Adelphi University, Ernie Zulia of Mill Mountain Theatre, James Spriggs of Karamu House, Tom Evans of Hanover College—*and*—Kurt Vonnegut, Jean Bepko, Adam Zahler, Henry Fonte, Jackie Manion.

To my parents, Ervin & Isabel,
who gave me the gift of life
and an indispensable sense of humor to go with it.

Contents

Foreword

These monologues serve three purposes. One, they provide actors with fresh, contemporary, powerful audition pieces that make a memorable impression at casting calls.

Two, they offer a sort of reportorial skeleton key by which actors may unlock a wide–ranging storehouse of inner emotion that will help them embody more fully a particular character or moment.

A monologue is a snapshot (sometimes vivid, sometimes blurry) that offers a fleeting glimpse into a human life at a particular passing instant in time. In essence, each of these monologues is a person, a person in a state of extreme transition or, possibly, bogged down forever in a situation of complete psychic paralysis.

They comprise a diverse span of characters: multi–cultural, multi–generational, often multi–personalitied individuals who are by turns confused, confident, bitter, ecstatic, depraved, shy, infinitely hopeful, irremediably hopeless. They are the world's winner and losers, the lucky and luckless, the sanctified and the hell–bound.

Some of the monologues are gender–specific; most can be used by female and male actors alike with slight alteration. Some are couched in the dialect of a certain social class or ethnicity. If you like the inherent idea or emotion, feel free to adapt the piece and character to your own interpretation.

And Purpose Number Three? Pure unadulterated entertainment—to sit back and relish the utter and total strangeness that is the constant and eternal wonder of life on this planet.

Be wild and well.

L.E. McCullough
Palenville Interarts Colony
Palenville, New York

Ice Babies in Oz

Strays

(female)

Well, like I told Herschell, I says, "I may be your wife—"

Say, how about a refill on that coffee, hon?

Anyways, I was down on West Washington last week walking to Mabel Flakmeyer's showing at the mortuary when I seen this cute little black lab.

Just a–setting on the steps of the trustees office all scared and wet and chilled to the bone.

Then a woman in the laundromat cross the street come over.

Said she saw somebody looked like in a rusted–out Chevy with a *I Love God Cause He Made Dolly Parton* bumper sticker just put that poor little hungry dog off at the corner, musta been two days ago.

So I took him back to my house and washed him and fed him and hugged him a bunch.

And named him Mr. Lucky.

And introduced him to Miss Maylene the born–again Siamese and Professor WonderBar the one–eared dachshund and Lady Madonna the talking blue budgie.

And all them six–toed calico kittens ain't got named yet.

Then when Herschell falls home round midnight after losing the poker tournament at the Purple Garter the fourth straight week, he says to me:

"Woman," he says—

"If I'da known you'd be spending all you damn time bringing in every damn stray on the West Side, I'da thought twice about moving in with you!"

"Herschell," I says:

"If I wasn't in the habit of taking in strays, I wouldnt'a thought twice about taking in you!"

I mean, after all, hon—you can pick up a good enough husband anytime.

But a good dog, well, now...

They just don't come along that often, you know.

The Rest Was History

(male)

It's funny the places you meet your women. Take my first ex–wife Jodie. Met her at an anti–war be–in concert at Military Park when I was sixteen and playing bass in a band called the Liberation Gypsy Jazz Orchestra, and we had had the band just long enough for everybody in it to get laid at least twice.

It was a strange time back then. It was a time when the first taste of freedom got you trapped in ways you could never figure out till it was too late.

Then ex–wife numero dos came into my life down in Texas when I saw her marching on an anti–pornography picket line out-side a 7–11 in San Antonio that stocked sex magazines within sight of children over thirteen accompanied by their parents. I'd stopped to get a sixpack of Lone Star and saw her carrying a sign said SEX BELONGS UNDER THE COVERS, NOT OVER THE COUNTER. I bought a quart of orange juice instead, picked up a sign that read VISUAL GRIME IS SEXUAL CRIME and rolled right in behind her. The rest was history.

As was our marriage after five months. Her family never was too keen on their little chatita being a Yankee's bride, and I never was real sure if it was a regular type romance with the right kind of regular romance type and style. All I know is, after leaving her that last night I got in my jeep and drove forty–two miles through a silverthaw gullywasher with traces of hail and neon past Seven Sisters, past Wolf Springs, past Edgar and Diablo and the all–nite baile grande at The Rockin' M with Ruben De Luna y Su Conjunto Muy Caliente, halfway almost to Dime Box and the Pandora cutoff before my arms shook loose from the steering wheel's shuddering embrace and my mouth finally stopped kissing the moon–flecked fog wisps teasing my cheeks like moist dancing fingers and linger-ing tequila sighs.

Next morning at Lil' Toots Lucky 7 Spot, after chorizo mexi-cano, two flour tortillas con arroz y frijoles and three cups of bad, bad coffee—the only thing I could taste was her.

Real Music Don't Come Outa Books

(female)

You can talk all the damn French you want, sugar, but you still ain't goin' nowhere. I'm right here where I'm *supposed* to be, and *you* don't need to go any more far than where *I* got you. Uh–huh. Yeh. Like this music school you–all think is so special. Well, let me tell you somethin's gonna hit you like a brick in the beeswax, Mister High–and–Mighty: real music don't come outa books.

It come outa tarpaper shacks with mud floors and the stink of hog piss on your clothes, and a flock of hungry children eatin' red clay dirt in their salt mush, 'cause the last time they had a taste of meat or fresh vegetables was the last time their daddy whupped their mama and caught the midnight train for Memphis one step ahead of the lynchin' tree.

That's real music, Sonny Boy Dupree, and it come from gettin' kicked in the gut every single day of your life and not givin' a damn, but gettin' up again and kickin' back and kickin' back and kickin' back and hollerin' just as loud as you can till your voice done screamed itself flat gone, cause there ain't nothin' else you can do!

Somebody, Please

(female)

Hello? Principals office, please. Yes, this is Jennifer M. Hollingsworth. I'm the mother of Brandon R. Hollingsworth the Third. He's a fourth–grader, I can't remember his teacher's name, we're new in the district—yes, yes, Lucianelli, that's it, Mrs. Lucianelli, yes, thank you. Listen, the reason I'm calling is, no, his midterm grades were very satisfactory, no, yes, penmanship can bear improvement, yes, that's not—yes, I'd be happy to set up a parent–teacher conference to discuss his—listen, please, I'm downtown at the courthouse, Domestic Relations Court, yes. The judge has just issued a bench warrant against Brandon's father for non–payment of child support. This is not the first time—what? His name is Brandon R. Hollingsworth, Junior. The father, yes. When this has happened in the past, he's come to the school and taken Brandon away and then—what? No, he does *not* have joint custody, he says he does, but that's not true. The divorce decree says he has to undergo family counseling before getting custody, but he never has and that was three years ago and—what? No, Brandon does not have to undergo counseling—what? Brandon, Junior, yes, the father, not my son Brandon. No. Yes. Please, what I'm telling you—is the principal in today? May I—could you—all right, please, listen, I'm at a pay phone and I'm late for work, please, listen, please, please. Please. The court has issued an arrest warrant for Brandon's father, Brandon R. Hollingsworth. *Junior.* Based on his past behavior I am warning you it is likely he will show up at school sometime this afternoon—yes, the sheriff has been notified and—no, I don't know if he's—you do have metal detectors? Yes, Brandon is at school today. No, my son Brandon. No, I don't want to talk to the security officer, I, yes, all right, no, yes, yes, yes—look, I just want to let somebody there know that if Mr. Hollingsworth shows up and tries to take our son—*my son*— from the school he *must* be stopped. He's very unstable and has a history—listen, please, listen. You've got to stop him. Please. Please. You have to. Please. Please, you have to stop him. You have to. Somebody has to. Somebody has to. Somebody, please. Please. Stop him. Please...

Hey You Sitting There Looking at This

(female/male)

HEY YOU SITTING THERE LOOKING AT THIS.
Look at the person next to you.
Go ahead.
Smile at them. No crime to smile on a bus.
Now say, "Hi."
Tell them your name.
Ask what they did at work today. Tell them something fun you did this week.
Ask how their family is. Tell him about the last poem you read.
Ask if they like porcupines. Tell them your thoughts on telepathy. Ask what their favorite food is and whether or not they were aware that the letters in Seattle also spell "Let's Eat".
Then tell them about the feeling you get when you stand on a street corner on a bright spring morning, and the wind riffles through your hair and gently touches your face and you remember you felt the wind exactly like this at another time, and the memory provokes an incredible mysterious feeling that just blows your mind cause you know it was something to do with something magical that happened or is about to perhaps.
Ask them if they believe in an Afterlife. And if they think this might be one.
I mean, somehow Fate has arranged it so that you got ten minutes five days a week to try and learn something unusual about another human instead of sitting there like a grease stain pretending you're invisible and deaf and nobody cares.
Maybe you'll make a new friend.
Or hear a new joke.
Or get kinda nervous and then real scared and maybe FREAK OUT and have to run for the police—*wow!*—cause the person you finally got up the guts to talk to is actually an escaped lunatic from the local cannibal condo, and they've got huge fangs ready to rip your inner organs to little–bitty shreds and and and—
Well. At least you'll be doing something more exciting than reading this silly pamphlet.

Club Lido, Kansas City, 1944

(female/male)

In the crumbling black–and–grey photograph my parents smile at each other across a cozy corner table at the Club Lido in Kansas City, 1944.

Two Norman Rockwell sweethearts holding hands and sipping cherry sodas like Adolf Hitler was some goofball sidekick on the Jack Benny Comedy Hour.

My father wears his officer uniform and a fresh army haircut. Grins adoringly at my mother, whose dark, snood–bound hair spills in lush waves across bare slender shoulders arches in a Rita Hayworth pinup pose.

I want to step into that photograph and walk up to their table and tell them about the new world coming round the corner like a rocket.

About Hiroshima, hula hoops, Howdy Doody and the blacklist. About JFK, SDS, cocaine babies, call waiting, Agent Orange and microwaves. About diet Coke and Chernobyl, tie–dyes and Elvis, one step for mankind, burn baby burn, Wheel of Fortune, glasnost and Star Wars.

And about all the hurt and pain they'll suffer as a matter of course from the children they dare to bring into this world.

Mostly I want to ask just how they can sit there and smile. And be so sure they'll still be smiling at each other this way half a century later.

When they don't even know Madonna's last name. Or the price of cherry sodas in the Year of the Fax.

Three Bears Lived in a Jungle

(male)

Some redheaded woman from Kentucky and her two kids and black dog drove up in a rusted out Toyota twodoor and moved into the old yellow woodframe cross the alley.

That was Tuesday.

Then Zettie's stepson Herschell got pissdrunk and plowed his damn Harley into a fencepost on 52 the day after.

I had to hock that VC k–bar I got at Vung Tau to raise his bail.

And when I come back I seen Riley Frazier the roofer got laid off come out of Roy's Recovery Room headed down the unemployment office with his ex–wife following behind screaming for her child support.

Then this morning one of them young kids from cross the way come over. A little skinny boy with peanut butter and jelly stains on his chin, dirty blue jeans tore out at both knees and his hair not washed proper you could tell.

Mister, he says. They got a new war on TV. And my momma, she gonna buy me and my baby sister Goddam Saddam t–shirts and a scud video game soon as our ADC check come in.

Hey mister, he says. Was you *born* in that wheelchair?

Son, I says. Set down on that box of empties right there, and I'll tell you a story.

About three bears lived in a jungle.

Mama–san, Papa–san and Baby–san...

Have a Nice Day

(female)

Biographically speaking I can't say much, other than I am of pure Dutch–Irish–Creole ancestry born in Mobile, Alabama and nearly murdered on a fetus–removal table in Denver nineteen years later.

Which is when I realized writing is essential to human life. My life in particular, because it has taught me who I am. What this world is about. And how maybe perhaps I can comprehend and survive and contribute positively to life on this planet.

My writing draws INSPIRATION–MANIA–POWER from: Janis Joplin. Lizzie Borden. Bette Davis. Queen Maeve. Miss Lulu Bett. And Squeaky Fromme... The Wayward Daughter Any–or–All–Of–Us Might Have Become if we'd worked hard enough at it.

And now I journal daily, largely undisturbed by cretins or dogmatics, in a small town outside of Indianapolis—capital of speed orgies and shrill penis–blinded preachers—with some of my words occasionally spilling into poem shapes, some into story shapes and of course others drifting into avenging Mad Medusa snake shapes, biting heads and taking names after much too long a polite silence, I mean, it's a wartime mission, sisters, and I will continue by whatever means possible and necessary until I die.

Have a nice day!

Sweet Blackberry Wine

(female/male)

(For Sonny Gholson, 1931–1993)
They called you blind, Mr. Piano Man.
But you could see into our hearts. Deep.
Past skin tone and fashion fad. Deep.
Past barroom cant and stoned soul supervibes. Deep.
Past skewed shards of dreams deferred, twisted lifeless in choking spasms of self–hate. Deep.

To where music born of Delta blood forged in steelblast rage and flew from fingers unfettered to glide smooth, smooth as a satin doll wadin' in the water all misty like stardust falling after hours on a night train rolling cross a midnight sun to the deep deep deep black bottoms.

Mr. Piano Man: every note you ever played saved somebody's soul.

Whether they knew it.

Needed it.

Or deserved it.

And, hey, man...you are *not* dead.

Cause you put enough music into this world to keep you—and everybody in it—ALIVE!

Till the river turns to whiskey, and muddy water tastes like sweet blackberry wine.

Ice Babies in Oz

(female)

My last job, I was working as a file clerk in a women's health clinic on Tremont. One day I went out for lunch and didn't go back.

It was strange, but I wasn't bothered by the ten–year–old in for her third procedure, sucking her thumb and squeezing a wornout teddy bear with no ears saying she knew her daddy really loved her and that's why he wanted her to have a little baby sister of her own.

Or having the preachers sit in the waiting room telling the girls just before they went in to sedation that if they didn't have this baby, God would make their breasts fall off and give them AIDS.

And the bomb threats that came in every hour or so—you got to joking around with them after awhile. They're bored and a lotta times scared, too, cause of the guilt and fear that eats away at their insides like a cancer, or the Sixth Plague of Egypt one woman said, sobbing into my ear.

Nope. It was the dreams I started having, sometimes two or three times a night, where I stood at the top of the Yellow Brick Road with Dorothy, who was in her second trimester and some-what pale and visibly nervous. We were going to walk up that road, me and Dorothy together, holding hands all the way up the road to visit the big jolly green Doctor of Oz.

And as we passed the Good Witch of the South practicing her Lamaze exercises, we saw little ice sculptures stuck in the snow by the side of the road. Bright glittery crystals shining and sparkling in all shapes and sizes and colors, stuck all along the road ahead of us just lining the road to Oz like glittery crystal mile markers along a candy rainbow interstate.

Then Dorothy started to yell and point, sinking to her knees like she was going to pass out. And I...I looked closer at one of the sculptures. And at another...and another...and saw they weren't crystals at all...but all tiny frozen munchkin fetuses with their little munchkin heads and faces all frozen up into smiles and giggles and grins.

Little heads and faces that smiled and giggled and grinned

and talked to me and Dorothy and said that they were really happy, cause now they would never ever have to go down on earth and get beat up or raped or killed in a war or be poor or lonely or hungry or insane like they would if they had to live a real human life in the real human world.

"We're the lucky one," they said to me in my dream. "We get to be happy little ice babies in Oz."

A Genuine Education President

(female/male)

Ladies and gentlemen, I'd like to be Your President.

Go on, laugh, laugh yourselves till you puke, go ahead.

But if [your name] were Your President, people, I would be the best kind of President there is.

I would be A Genuine Education President.

I would teach our children what they must learn in order to survive in this modern fiber–optic world.

I would teach them that rich people will beg you for your last dollar. And kick your butt off a cliff if they think they got it.

I would teach them that smart bombs ain't so smart. They kill good people along with the bad and don't even know the difference *or* know enough to care.

I would teach them that minute rice cooks best in an hour. And to beware the man whose mouth is so big he can eat a banana sideways.

And never turn your back on the man who will do anything for the workers except become one. Or the woman who's had a seven–year itch the last two months.

I'd tell them to never turn a deaf ear to a blind date.

And wear rubber soles if you're going to run through rain-drops.

And *always* let sleeping dogs lie, especially if they're at the bottom of a swimming pool.

I'd tell them not to worry about making the same mistake twice when you can still find ways to make a new one. And to never forget that old men are two times a boy with one–half the sense, and that fools and children always speak the truth...unless they heard it from a lawyer or a preacher

And always, *always* remember that there is no truth without justice.

And there is no justice without the money to buy it.

Vote for me!

Early and often, if you please.

Jump Start

(male)

You're dang lucky I'm a good mechanic, sonny. You got a leaky bovine insulator valve, and, lemme tell you, a bad BIV is not bucket of grins, as you just found out. How often you service this vehicle? Looky there. See that squarish thingamabob by the distributor? That's your thermohyperbole aerator. And that bronze wire alongside? Your libido intake coupler. Looks a mite threadbare to me. Over by the fuel pump...there's the scruple armature. And the divinity differential right there beside it, um–hmm. I'd have the decorum by pass manifold checked out, they can snap on you in a hard freeze, and it wouldn't do one bit of harm to clean out your secondary infatuation sensor with some good, old–fashioned Burmashave.

You know, sonny, a hundred years ago a car was a conveyance. A simple horseless carriage. An extension of a natural flesh–and–blood function performed by natural flesh–and–blod creatures. Then people started buying cars for other reasons. For status. For self–esteem. For sex. Cars got more complicated till with computers and whatall, your basic automobile's got more working parts and systems than the human body. It's become a creature of its own with its own intelligence that grows by leaps and bounds every passing day.

How much time you spend behind the wheel, sonny? Hmmm, that much, eh? Well....

Figure in your trips to the grocery, drycleaners, bank machine, video store, and the average person, even a little kid, spends almost half their waking hours absorbing the car's L.F.P.R.— "Life–Force Particle Radiation" to you and me. Guess you'd call it the *soul* of the car. Humans these days are chock fulla tension and phobias and psychotic episodes and repressed anxieties from their childhood, and it all mingles in with your car's life–force. That's why most cars get outa whack so quick. See that big generator of mine? Got extra juice to restore the life–force balance. Ratio should be about 60–40, especially with this greenhouse effect we got nowadays.

Don't like to brag, sonny, but one glance under the hood and I know exactly what ails a person's soul. A broke–down axle or a busted fan belt ain't just a piece of metal or rubber gone bad...corresponds to some strained part of your psyche, a part of your spirit that's sick or twisted or about ready to go haywire and do you permanent damage.

Remember this. All the traveling you do represents your progress through life. When you figure out where it is you really need to go, you'll find the car that gets you there. All righty. Hop in and fire up. I got another call comin' in.

Plenty of Time

(female/male)

I took the boy down to Methodist to see his mother yesterday. She's been on suicide watch and some detox, too, since Tuesday.

When we got to the bus stop, we saw an Asiatic girl, a college student at the University most likely, reading one of her school books and sitting there real small and slim and flowery–like, with long straight black hair shimmering like liquid black marble and floating a little wavy bit in the cool morning breeze.

Then a big fat kid come up, a teenager in torn blue jeans, black spike boots and dirty white teeshirt with ARYAN AVENGERS painted on it. Didn't even look at me or the boy but just spit on the ground right next to the girl's feet and yelled:

"Know what you are? Goddam slant eyes so goddam smart IQ can't even talk goddam English!"

The girl closed her *Readings in American History* book, a fine wisp of soft marble black hair dangling across pink parted lips, and looked up at him real slow, studying him a second or two like he was a strange kinda bug just lit on her lunch:

"My eyes see you, sir, very well. You, sir, are A Racism."

Then she went back to reading her book, and the teenager cussed a few more seconds and spit again and finally stalked off down the street trying to kick an empty beer can but missing by a good half a foot.

The bus come about a minute later, and all the way down-town I could tell the boy was upset and not likely just by his mother.

I mean, there's plenty of time before he gets older till he's expected to hate people for no damn reason at all.

Campfire Girl

(male)

I told the story about Clifford Heitelspaum and the new wait-ress from French Lick to Cashondra that night hoping to get in a better mood, and she laughed and said:

Men. They marry you, then leave you by the campfire like an old Indian squaw, tending their babies, cooking their meals, inflat-ing their drooping egos and penises, picking up after them day in year out, always cleaning up their goddam mess while they run off to the woods waving their pricks and your checkbook at women they don't have to marry.

I know, I said. I know just what you mean. Women with plush two–tone thighs and sleek retractable radial breasts, spanking new showroom model high–performance women they keep tanned and chromed and ultra–waxed, tuned up for weekend road rallies with the guys who've already forgotten you—a boring, broken old junker parked out of sight in the garage next to the catbox with the other old stuff they're too embarrassed to admit ever gave them anything more than a few laughs and some inconvenient children.

But you know what? I said. Me—I *like* campfires.

I like watching the glowing embers caper in the ashes and leap with gleeful yowls into the vanishing curtain of midnight blackness.

I like the way the slender nimble orange flamefingers reach into the air and sketch deft pictures of nymphs and goddesses dancing across eons and galaxies, twisting and weaving to the flut-ing sorcery of laughing Pan whistling his songs of seduction in the cool night breeze.

Most of all I like how the soft flickering shadowlight pulls me into your eyes where your tender gaze tells me that here is where I must spend the night, tonight and every night from now until the sun expires and day becomes night.

Forever—

Just the two of us dancing with fire nymphs, soaring to the music of a goat god and watching our lives dwindle and sink lov-ingly into soft slumbering ashes.

Just me and my campfire girl.

Partners Forever

(male)

Hey, man, wanna drink? Hey, I'm Staker Wallace, remember me? That's right, I'm out on my own now. I'm a solo act, that's right, you dig it. No, uh–uh, I don't play with Sonny Boy Dupree no more. Doin' too much fancy stuff. Too much merde!

Yeh, hey, baby, hey, baby, you know ol' Staker, yeh, there, baby, how's your poodle, baby, how's your poodle? Hey, you know, I feel a whollllllllle lot better since I been playin' on my own, you know that? I mean, he was keepin' *me* down, know what I mean?

Damn you, Sonny Boy Dupree! I can hear you...right now...yes, I can...you just messin' with me! I know you, you just messin' with me! Think you gonna throw ol' Staker away like a used–up toothpick! Well, merde on you! Go merde all over the whole damn world, you want! But, you remember this...we partners...now and forever!

It's This Rain

(female)

It's this rain.

Yes, that's what it is. The rain. It reminds me...of when I was a little girl...after my parents...

We had just moved to an old part of an old city. Big old grey houses with big creaky porches and big empty windows staring out at the street, surrounded by big grey iron fences all tangled up with dead grey vines. Everything big and old and grey and dead.

It rained every day. Grey rain. Seeping and dripping and drizzling and oozing and sliding down your forehead onto your nose, into your eyes, your ears, your lips, your chin...little streams of dead grey water plopping down on top of your skull, stinging your face, smacking your hands, pounding your shoulders and punching the back of your neck and back like a hard wet mop head. Pushing and probing and poking at you so you couldn't look up but had to always look down, always look down at the old grey puddles oozing out of them, and as you walked you could see yourself in the puddles. *In* the puddles, like you were looking at yourself inside the puddle, inside the scar, inside where there was a person trapped, and the person was you inside the puddle, and you could see yourself getting pounded and punched and poked by the rain hitting down at you, but you couldn't look up because the further away from home you walked the puddles got bigger and deeper and harder until they rose up at the corner where the big sewer drain was and the pavement cracked and sloped down toward the drain which was gushing with water flowing from the puddles in which you could see yourself getting washed away through the puddle down the drain into the sewer, and no matter how hard you ran or how loud you screamed and screamed and screamed and screamed screaming you were falling into the puddle and drowning in the water and sliding down the drain into the sewer and into the darkness, the water stinging and smacking and pounding and punching and pushing and poking and gushing over your head up your nose in your eyes the sewer opened up like a big ugly scar gushing and screaming screaming screaming, pounding and punching, pounding and punching, screaming and screaming...

...what?

I don't know. You're the shrink. It was an accident. I mean, just cause I don't like rainy days doesn't mean I'd let my own baby drown in her bathtub. Does it?

Patient Hands

(female)

Well, Edwina, you say what you want, but take that piano player, Sonny Boy Dupree. Mmmm–mmm–mmmmm...his hands are really something else.

First off, a piano–playing man has got patient hands. Patient, smooth hands with easy fingers. Easy and strong, from riding up and down those ivories, sometimes fast and crazy like a puppy dog chasing its tail round and round...sometimes reallllllll slowwwwwwww when they come to a special spot in the music, a special tender spot, and stop and linger awhile right there, mmm–hmm, and keep lingering and lingering and lingering some more, teasing a little bit, uh–huh, mmm–hmm, maybe tickle even—heh–heh–heh, oh, you know, get away, get away, go on—but always so warm and gentle and tender and mmm–mmm–mmm delicious, oh don't stop, don't stop, don't stop! Ohhhhhh...ohhhhhh...ohhhhhh...

Course, a man like Sonny Boy Dupree...he's got *busy* hands. They want to jump on top of *every* piano they bump up against. whether she's a shiny slick uptown baby grand...or a fallen–apart, stumpy–legged pile of rusty knobs and strings.

What, child? No, you don't need a man that's superior to you, baby.

Just one that's richer.

A New Generation

(male)

Traitors! Traitors! You're all goddam CIA goddam traitors!

Hey–hey, CIA, how many babies ya kill today!

Hey, I *know* who killed John Kennedy! Hey, goddammit! Don't you ever watch television? Huh? Channel D, channel D for Death! Jesus H. Watergating Christ, the goddam FBI's had my phones tapped for years. Years!

If it was worth going to, I've been there. On the front lines. At the barricades. Mississippi, 1964. Berkeley, 1965. Chicago, '68. Chile, '71. Johannesburg '73. And now...Suburban Milwaukee, in the Bicentennial Year of Our Lord Gerry Ford, 19 and 76! (sings) Oh, I'm a Yankee Doodle Dandy...

You don't know my fans, little brother. They are a *New* Generation. They are dedicated, they are committed, they are warriors in the fight against fascism.

They are dancing their butts off to bad bad disco.

Amigo, you are the best buddy a washed–up poet without a voice could ever hope for, a great white hope in a family of baa–baa black sheep, have you any wool! (sings) Yes, ma'am, no ma'am, two days' full...

But you know what?

You're bringing me *down,* goddamit! I'm an artist! Don't bother me with mundane details of commerce! I'm a poet, not a goddam accountant! Now get outa here so I can think for five seconds!

Credit Check

(female/male)

Mr. Nelson, we live in a world defined by one simple, universal law: the law of supply and demand. When the global population reached eighteen billion at the turn of the century, the world's corporate and political leaders realized there simply wasn't enough of the quote–unquote "good life" to go around. If *any* of us were to enjoy the shrinking pool of material assets and social amenities, access had to be *limited*...strictly limited to those members of society who truly *deserved* that access.

It became imperative that every *minute,* every *second* of human effort be dedicated toward creating a more productive, hence more perfect world. Do you recall your Bible, Mr. Nelson? Third Gospel of St. Trump, may he earn in peace, amen, The Book of The Deal, I'll paraphrase here: "Life is a precious social resource that can no longer be left to the mere individual to piss away."

Fortunately, Mr. Nelson, our report shows you are a model citizen living an exemplary life. A morally–prudent, economically–fertile American life.

Customer Number 308–52–4156–8417, your credit check has been completed, and we are pleased to approve your application for additional credit at this time. Your good credit has earned you one more year of life! With a preferred customer bonus of an extra four months, seventeen days and thirteen hours.

No, no, don't thank *us*, Mr. Nelson—thank *you* for using First National Life & Loan, America's premier life–equity specialists. Remember, at First National, you can trust your family's life span to us. Millions already do. Millions already do. Millions already do. Millions already do. Millions already do...

The Flames of Hell

(female/male)

The talent agent man snaps his fingers and the Cadillac start up, motor racing and lights all ablaze. Then *bazzam!*—the Cadillac *and* the talent agent man with the bright red walking stick were gone, just in the instant you blink your eye, cher—not a trace of the man or his car but a thin puff of black, black smoke twisting slowly through the live oak trees and cypress.

"Hooowheeee!" say young Aldus, rubbing one eye then another, then both at the same time to make sure this is not some kind of dream, and he is not really in his own bed at home.

"Don't that beat all! Aiieee! No more squirrel jambalaya and gaspergou gumbo *pour moi! Quelle chance*, there is the sun about ready to rise itself. I best get back in my pirogue and go on to home."

But now, in the bright light of the waking dawn, when Aldus picks up his accordion, what do you think but there were two big burn marks on either side of the bellows...burn marks like big flames...or huge big burning hands—right where that talent agent man had squeezed it.

"Mon dieu de tout le monde!" cry Aldus, as each finger of each hand burned into the accordion was in the shape of an animal claw—not an alligator or grizzly or puma, cher—but something almost human, yet too much more horrible to ever imagine meeting by your lonesome in the middle of the dark bayou.

And when Aldus got back to his home and show his accordion to his family and neighbors, they all say, "These, monsieur, these are the flames of hell. That talent agent man who tempt you was the devil, and these be his mark...the mark he was hoping to put upon your eternal soul."

Shiver

(female/male)

I woke up in the middle of the night and heard momma's and Barry's voices. I could hear they were both in her room but couldn't hear any words and fell back asleep and dreamed Barry and momma had got married and we were on a honeymoon cruise around the world somewhere in the South Pacific.

I'd dreamed this dream a lot that summer, but this time Barry was next to me at the helm, and it was night with a big orange full moon peeking through a curtain of dark clouds being swept along by a stiff northeasterly breeze that had just enough push to send a shiver through you when you weren't expecting it, which made it an even stranger kind of shiver than a just plain cold breeze shiver.

A shiver that had fingers and hands and a voice to it almost that spoke your name like it had known you a good long while and was going to touch and talk to you whenever it wanted whether you wanted it to or not, like a strange growly dog tailing you down the street you weren't sure was following to be a friend, or maybe was going to bite you if it had the chance, but you couldn't make it go away until it wanted to itself.

The wind gusted stronger, and all of a sudden I sense we were off course. I looked at Barry, and he was plenty worried. "Get below with your mother!" he yelled. "And put on your life jackets!" I looked for momma but couldn't find her where I thought she was and couldn't hear her singing but only the voice of the wind shiver whispering at the back of my head, though I couldn't understand a word, and the shiver–voice got louder, but I still couldn't hear any words and grabbed a life jacket and called momma's name but got no answer just as the boat gave a terrible lurch and I slammed into the tool cabinet but got to my feet and staggered back up to the deck where momma was standing at the helm and the rain slashing down in big windy sheets as she stood at the helm not steering but with her hands wrapped around her and her face hidden by the wind.

"Where's Barry?" I shouted, but she didn't look at me and didn't answer. "Where's Barry?" I screamed again, and I started calling his name until the rain pounded out my screams, and I slipped and tumbled across the slippery deck and got caught in the rigging of a fallen sail and heard the shiver–voice laugh like a cruel bully and then I woke up and found myself on my bedroom floor, legs all twisted up in the snarled topsheet and half the pillowcase jammed in my mouth.

We never, either of us, saw Barry again.

Guardian Angel

(male)

So a couple of weeks ago I'm drivin' my car through the West Side, okay? Got the top down, good cruisin' music on the tapedeck, clear sailin' all down the avenue. I'm goin' through the intersection on the green and *wham!*—I almost get hit by this old woman rammin' through on a red 'cept I managed to brake at the last second. *She* just keeps zippin' along, but I get a glimpse of her—orange hair piled up in a beehive, huge gold earrings shaped like donuts and a bright blue scarf around her neck. And as I'm quiverin' from the sudden traumatics of the situation, I recall a couple months ago the same thing happenin' to me at a light on the *East* Side. And I could swear the other yahoo what nearly bonked me was the *same* old lady with the same orange hair and same crazy earrings and same scarf, just like she dropped down outa the sky or somethin'.

Couple days later, I'm strollin' down 10th Street, somebody shouts my name. I look up and there is a big brown shape of somethin' gettin' bigger and bigger and comin' straight at me. I step aside, and *bazoomba!*—this giant jumbo blueberry bagel size of a German Shepherd smashes into the pavement and busts the sidewalk to pieces after missin' my noggin by like this much. Eight, nine floors above, there's a face stickin' out the window, and it's *her!* The old babe with the hair and the earrings and the damn scarf, and then *zipporama!*—she's gone. I'm quiverin'.

Next week, I'm in Altoona. Never been in Altoona in my entire life. I walk into a diner, sit at the counter, order a ham–and–cheese with a big side of slaw. It comes, I dig in and discover to my dismay, a two–inch piece of broken glass buried in the slaw. I look up at the serving window, there is my chum—Mrs. Donut Ears. I tell the waitress, "I gotta give my compliments to the chef," *juzook!*—I'm back in the kitchen where I see the old dame sittin', sharpenin' a butcher knife.

"I dunno why you're always tryin' to kill me," I says. "You a friend of my ex–mother–in–law?"

"I'm your guardian angel," she says. "And I been keepin' you from dyin' accidentally. Every time you see me, it means you coulda got killed but didn't, cause I got your attention at the last second. That slaw you ordered was bad and gonna give you fatal food poisoning."

"Look," I says. "I'm tired of bein' spied on alla time. If I gotta buy the big one, so be it. Why doncha just lemme croak in peace? *Pazapparooni!* Instant total death!"

"Instant total death?" she says, then calls out to the cook. "Sammy, gimme a Number 3 blue plate, extra mayo and cheese whiz. Oh, and, mister—pay the cashier on the way back to your seat. In this establishment it's customary to pay *before* bein' served.

The Twelve Commandments

(male)

And I'm telling you, Harley, the last thing this town needs is an outbreak of religious tolerance. You remember the last time there was a preacher in Duckburg? Back before the Citizens' Civic Reform Committee rode the last one out on a rail. Why, back then there was no more than four or five juke joints in the county, even with all the suckers—er, soldiers—on leave from the war.

And today, you can walk from right here in downtown Duckburg in any direction for half a mile, and there's more jukes than you can count on your short hairs.

You see, Harley, the problem with preachers is they get people thinking too damn much about worthless notions like heaven and hell. Right and wrong. Sin and salvation. Whoa, now, mister, don't you go get it in your mind Mayor Samuel T. Applebung is some no–good communistic New York City atheist that don't believe in God or the Twelve Commandments. Nosir, I am crucially well–informed upon the subject of religion. As the Bible says, "What does it profit a man to save his soul and lose his mistress in a poker game?"

An Incredibly Lucky Man

(female/male)

After Daddy died, you persuaded your younger brother Jonathan to quit high school and take a job to put you through college.

You were going to be a smart, modern agriculturalist and make the farm healthy again. Make Momma healthy again. You promised Jonathan you'd work to pay his college when you graduated.

But when it came time to return his generosity, you had other ideas, didn't you?

Ah, yes, the impulsive ideas of impractical youth! *You* refused to pay Jonathan back. Or give him any money for college. Instead, you squandered *his* earnings gambling and courting high–society chippies from Tarrytown. "A&M will still be there in a year or two," you told him. "You've got a good job in the fertilizer factory. Keep working."

And you stole his car. And his fiancée. And you went to California, to embark on an undistinguished career of thieving, pimping, swindling and total moral degeneracy!

Ah, yes...you *wanted* to get the money to pay him back. To earn his forgiveness. But everything *you* did turned to failure, everything *he* did turned to success. Yes, yes, your brother is an incredibly lucky man.

Hah! Seventy–two years old and still making excuses about luck. Pity. When will you ever admit the truth? Your brother's ambition was fueled by his complete and utter hatred for you.

I Wasn't Always Like This

(male)

Ladies and gentlemen...fellow F Train commuters: I don't wanna disturb anybody. But I really need your help.

Anything you can spare. A dollar. A bagel. A cigarette. A condom, preferably unused. I mean, you really need all that stuff in your purse, lady? Jesus, a family of five could live in there! Whatsit have a garage and a sauna in the lower level?

Okay, okay. Hey, I wasn't always like this. But you know that. I had more money than alla yous on this train. Yeh, I was a CEO of a major medical research corporation. Uh–huh. Okay, okay. I made that up. I was a boxer took a bad punch. I was a stock broker took a bad tip. I was a bricklayer got hit by a ton of bricks. I was a missionary got eaten by cannibals. I was a rock star, a rocket scientist, a rockette at Radio City Music Hall—hey, whatsit matter? I'm a human be–ing! Huh? Look at me! Look at me, mister! Yeh, I'm *you*. Next week. Next month. Next year. Next life. Take a good look, why doncha? Look into my eyes, and see *you*!

Okay, okay, I don't wanna disturb anybody. But I really need your help. Anything you can spare. A cookie. A coupon. A dead cigar, preferably Cuban. Hey, I ain't proud. I'll be your personal recycling center. Give me your kleenex, your paper clips, your huddled pocket lint yearning to be free! This is America, dammit, and I demand freedom of pocket lint! I demand all the pocket lint you people are gonna throw away down the sewer same way you try to throw me away, throw me away like some throw me away away like some goddam some goddam throw me down the goddam constitution Thomas Jefferson Iwo Jima Benedict Arnold I never told a goddam lie stinking cherry tree I ain't got but one sock to give for mmmmmy counnnnn–ry tisssss of theeeeee, sweet lllllland offfff I know the President, Mrs. Eisenhower, personally, you know—

Whupp. Whoa. Okay, okay, we're pulling into 53rd Street, midtown. Watch your step, watch your step. Thank you, maam, thank you. Anybody got a light?

This Corner My Bidness

(male)

This here my corner. You got that right, young mama. This be my corner seventeen, no eighteen year. Right here on the cool, shady side. Ain't nobody, no mayor, no po–lice, no president gonna get me offn it neither, nosir. Sixth and Neches, yessir, you can find Delford B. Washington, Esquire, right here regular as, say what?

Purlie? Purlie? Don't know no Purlie? Don't know nobody name Purlie round here. Perry. You mean Perry. Dude name Perry. White dude. Now what is his last name? Met him when he first come to town. From Shreveport. Uh–huh. Owned a hardware store up there. Lost it in a di–vorce case. That be bout all I know.

You a de–tective, heh–heh? Lady de–tective? Plainclothes? Uh–huh. Won't go no farther this corner, nosir. I mind my own bidness, babe. You mind *your* bidness, I mind *my* bidness. Don't *you* try mind *my* bidness...I mind *my* bidness, hear? Now this cor-ner *my* bidness. Say, you lookin' good, you know that? Say, you wanna...hold on...where you goin'...say, mamma, hey...hold on...

Our Most Requested Attraction

(male)

Good morning, madam, this is Friendly Frank's World of Mega–Talent Entertainment Connection, Frank speaking. How may we assist in serving your entertainment needs this fine day?

Excuse me? I'm sorry, madam, but Mister Dinky the Clown from Outer Gonzo Land is our *most* requested attraction—yes, I believe Mister Dinky *has* had his rabies and distemper shots—excuse me? He did *what* at your son's birthday party? Look, lady, Mister Dinky is a mature adult responsible for his own actions, he—he, *what*? Yes, he's been out on parole almost six weeks, how many times do I have to tell you—huh? What? Oh, *yeh*? Well, you can stick your whoop–dee–doo contract up your—hey, I don't care what, look, hey, it's not my fault, okay? Look, I know he was sup- posed to take his anti–psychosis medicine *before* the kid's party, right, it's in the contract, sure, sure, I know, but the meds make him shaky, which is not good for the knife–juggling part of the show—huh?—don't worry, a little bleach takes out those blood stains on the carpet—he *what*? So he dropped his drawers in front of a few little brats, sure, sure, so they'll all kill their mothers when they reach puberty, sure go ahead sue, go ahead sue me, bla–bla–bla–bla–bla–bla–bla–bla, and drove his unicycle through your very expensive designer crystal collection, sure, sure, right, and did *what* to your poodle? Ha–ha–ha! Yes, I think that's funny. I think it's hilarious, yeh, go on, go on, go on—huh? You and whose army, you old prune–sucking, booger–snarfing—hang on, hang on, I got another call coming in...

Good morning, sir, this is Friendly Frank's World of Mega–Talent Entertainment Connection, Frank speaking. How may we assist in serving your entertainment needs this fine day?

A fifieth wedding anniversary at St. Bridget's Parish Hall for a very sedate, very religious couple? Let me suggest the perfect fam- ily entertainer: Father McDinky the Golden Tenor from Tipperary is our *most* requested attraction. I'll just check his calendar...he's been traveling with the Pope in Argentina this past month on a wine–tasting tour of Northern Antarctica...

Your Mama She Lookin' Real Fine

(male)

Hey, how's your mamacita, cholo? She been workin' at the Denny's on 31 two, three weeks, now, huh? Man, I like that place. They got good eats, huh? Hey, you wanna see somethin' really boss? Check this out, my man. Know what that is, man? Take a guess. Go on. It's a lectrostaphic paint dispensin' machine, man, yeh, it shoots the paint out real clean, and when I get it fixed I'm gonna use it to put a new coata cherry flake on that toilet seat over there when I get it put back on. Now I got to get that water pump for that frigerator runnin', man. I been workin' on *it* for three–four weeks now, man, it been takin' a whollle lot outa me. But I'm gonna whup it, yeh I am, cause you got to take pride in your work, you known what I'm sayin'? I seen one like it one time in job corps. Hey, I learned a lotta stuff in job corps, man, wholle lotta stuff. I mean, it set me straight for life, know what I'm sayin'? I'm only nineteen but, hey, I got it together. You should check it out when you get ready for a career, man. Hey, you ever seen a thing like this here? Say what? You gotta go? Hey, man, you tell your mama she lookin' real fine, yeh, hey, tell her I said so, okay? Later, man.

Get a Grip

(male)

Hey, you think I talk on this phone for my goddam health? Yeh, I'm angry! I'm furious! I'm berserk! I'm a m–m–m–m–m–maniac! *Aaaaauuughgh!!!*

Hey, pal, I wanna scream at you on the goddam phone, I'm gonna scream at you on the goddam phone. Why? Whyyyyyyyy? You gonna try and stop me? Got a big gun, pal? Gonna reach through the phone line and kill me? Huh? Ever killed anybody before, pal? Huh? Yeh, sure. You couldn't kill your toenail with a frog staple! *Aaaaauuughgh!!!*

You know, pal, it's people like you that really frost my potato chips. I mean, where...do...you...get...*off*? This planet is headed toward total destruction in a matter of minutes. Yeh, that's right. Cataclysmic, absolute, utter and complete obliteration! And you're worried about how the Federal Reserve interest rate and the price of bananacide in Zimbabwe is gonna affect your revolving charge account at Montgomery Ward? Get...a...*grip*! Whatta you gonna do when you get launched into the Big Bang? The Cosmic Cuisinart. The Galactic Garbage Disposal. The Universal Everlasting Psychedelic Mother of All Space–Time Continuum Warp Blender's gonna shoot your gumbeenies into the Forever Hereafter without so much as a weasel fart.

And lemme tell you somethin' else, pal: it's all *your* fault. Why? Whyyyyyyyy? Cause you've lost faith. Yes, you've lost faith, you've lost hope, you've lost vision, you've lost direction, you've lost morality, you've lost your library card. You know where your library card is right now? Huh? Huh? Huh? C'mon, c'mon, c'mon, where's your damn library card? Nope, not in your wallet. Not in your pocket. Not in your dentures. Can't find it, can you, pal? Ha–ha–ha! Hey—you can't find your library card, mister, how you gonna save The Univerrrrrrssssse!!!

Aaaaauuughgh!!!
Aaaaauuughgh!!!
Aaaaauuughgh!!!

What? Beg pardon, ma'am? You wanna use this phone booth? Sure, here. It's okay, I ain't talkin' to nobody. I just like screamin'.

That Odor Again

(female)

Anyway I was very polite and invited him to Alamo House Tuesday. I think he wants to pork me...he just has that look they get—oh *god*! I don't need more silly men jumping my bones! I mean Greg laid *such* a heavyduty guilt trip when I canceled our date for tonight. An animation film festival—big deal.

A reverse guilt trip actually. "Practice? Practice? You're really good, Jana, you don't have to practice so much. You should step back from it now and then and keep a fresh perspective. It's making you tense. You're too close to it, step back."

Oh, he is *so* shrewd! Okay, I mean, okay, sure of course I'm tense maybe at times but that's where the inspiration comes from...you've got to have tension to create...tension is *it*! I mean if you don't have an edge, if you're not close to it okay I mean...I mean I just don't think he has a real grip on what it's about...on what *I'm* about...but it's just too draining...writing is the priority now that's all there is to it, I just had to tell him hey, look, man, it's over, I mean, okay, it looked really promising for a while, but lately you're so...so...so *hostile,* really, underneath the white–knight–concern–thing I mean, really, I mean you just don't seem to be even remotely aware of what I'm doing or what's happening with me at this point in my life, I mean...it's like I'm not a real personality to you anymore. I'm a void you want to fill up with yourself—all four inches, hah!—and squeeze out every thing in *me* that isn't *you*. I'm sorry, but I went through that whole male control thing with Glen for six years and uhhhhhh, *god*, there's that *odor* again! I'm calling the landlord right now!

So Help Me

(male)

Raise your right hand, class, and repeat after me:

I pledge allegiance to my agent, for he is the mightiest deal-maker in the land.

He will taketh my talent and maketh it yield a humongous annual net income I could never have conceivably pulled down without his expert assistance.

Yea, though I walk through the Valley of Slimeball Hustlers, I will fear not the Sharpies nor the Weasels nor the Scumbuckets competing for my contract.

Lo, I will rejoice in the power of my agent to secure lucrative syndication rights and foreign licensing deals in all major markets, and I will not begrudge him his commission, his...hmmmm...his, let's see, his thirty–five, no, that's too high, too high...his twenty–five, no, no, that's too low, his, let's see, his, right, his, no, wait, I've got it, I've got it, his pathetically meager but extremely well–deserved thirty–one–and–a–half percent commission—plus five to seven points, that's negotiable, of course—of all total gross revenues exclusive of any legal and compensatory expenses in conjunction with his actions on my behalf—or those of my assigned designates, heirs, proxies or loansharks—so help me da–da–da till bankruptcy or hostile takeover do us part.

Amen.

Key Word

(female/male)

As your attorney, Mr. Tubbernitz, I'd like to remind you that the key word in this situation is "fear".

Fear is a key word, Mr. Tubbernitz. Fear is your friend. Always think fear.

You've got to project an image of absolute invincibility. Make the other guy squirm. Sweat. Shrivel.

You've got to go in there thinking this guy has just killed your mother. Buggered your pet bunny rabbit. Bound and gagged your favorite tootsie roll and stuffed it down the sewer without so much as a single fare–thee–well or "Oops, that was an accident, I beg your pardon!"

And now...and now you're gonna nail his heiny to the wall with a rusty staple gun no matter what it takes!

Pressure, Mr. Tubbernitz, pressure. You have to keep up the pressure every second. Unbearable pressure. Make the other guy crack like an egg! Take no prisoners. Hit 'em with everything you got! Harder! Harder! Hit 'em again! Hit 'em again! Harder! Harder!

Yes, Mr. Tubbernitz, I'm glad to hear we have your complete confidence. We appreciate that. We appreciate your confidence. And trust, Do we have your trust?

Absolutely, you say? Absolutely without a doubt? Now, is that "absolutely without a doubt," Mr. Tubbernitz? Or is it "without a doubt absolutely"?

Come, come, sir! It's a crucial distinction, and the success of your case is hanging in the balance—pardon? Good. Excellent.

We appreciate your trust. And your confidence. And your fear.

Home Again

(male)

Then one day in '89 I was laying drunk outside a flop house in Mexicali thinking which one of the cantinas I'd visit that night when I heard that old Son House song *Death Letter Blues* on some loco homeboy's boombox. And the melody was like a long, long, long railroad track clickity–clack clickity–clack that picked me up and carried me along allllll along clickity–clack clickity clack through the years wayyyyy back to when I was six years old and sitting in Victory Field on 16th Street.

I was with my dad high up in the bleachers watching the Indians play Oklahoma City—*here's the windup...and the pitch...swish! crack! going back going back going wayyyyy back...it's outa here!* And it was the last time I remember ever seeing him, cause he left at the seventh–inning stretch to get us some hot dogs and root beer. And he just never came back. Not that day or the next. Not never.

And the more I kept listening to that song, the more I knew I had to come home here to Stringtown. A voice kinda like that ballpark announcer's voice spoke to me through that song and said, "Attention, you drunken piece of helpless baboon dung: you *need* to be back home again in Indiana not cause you know what you're gonna do there, but cause you don't know what you're gonna do any damn place else, so you might as well be ignorant and unknowing where people can at least look at you and say, 'Damn—I know that ignorant and unknowing yahoo. Hell, I went to grade school with him!'"

Only 159.95

(female)

You know, Delbert, I wish that for just one hour God would grant us a genu–wine miracle—giving you enough sense of smell to realize how much a room fulla cat pee really really *really* stinks.

I mean, good lord almighty, darlin', you cannot imagine what these cats have done! They've taken a perfectly good deluxe double–wide customized trailer ranchette and made it into their own private catbox. Have you maybe noticed how nobody wants to come over here and visit us no more? Have you maybe noticed how the postman always leaves our mail at the neighbors—two miles down the road? Have you maybe noticed how all the houseplants have up and died? Have you maybe noticed how all the curtains have disintegrated? Have you maybe noticed how your favorite salad dressing has that extra special unique flavoring of late?

Yes, I love cats, Delbert–honey, but why do we have to have so many of 'em? Say what? Fourteen cats is not "so many"? You know, darlin', they got a name for what's wrong with you. Yes, they do. I don't know what it is, but they do. And it is *serious*. Delbert, these animals are not "little fluffy furry people"—these are registered agents of chemical warfare!

God help me, I don't know why I even—Delbert, I am hip–deep in kitty doo–doo, and it is *everywhere*. In the sock drawer, behind the television, underneath the dishwasher...good god almighty, lookit this...there's a big yellow puddle in my blue mascara!

Say what? Must be my imagination? Well, imagine *this*...

This is a little something I bought today—a new miracle cleansing device guaranteed to rid us of our embarrassing odor problem once and for all. *Vvvvoooosshhhh!* That's right, darlin'—a genu–wine U.S. Army house–and–garden flamethrower! On sale at Wal–Mart for only 159.95. *Vvvvoooosshhhh!* Hoooweee, lookit that baby flare up! Assembled it myself while you were at the Tri–State Cat and Kitten Expo—and you said I wasn't mechanically minded. *Vvvvoooosshhhh!* Here, kitty, kitty... *Vvvvoooosshhhh!* Here, kitty...Delbert, you stand back now...we're gonna have barbecued furburgers for supper. Just set the table and put out the mustard. *Hoooweee!*

Garbage Don't Cry

(female/male)

It was early, sun not quite up. Broadway was looking good. Found a sweater, almost new. Three two–liter soda bottles in the gutter—that's a bagel and hot chocolate. Pair of gloves by the bus stop, had two fingers missing, otherwise okay. Gotta stock up with winter coming. Behind the deli on 112th was a fresh bag of corned beef. Mustard and mayo, not my favorite, either, but if it ain't crawling, I'll eat it.

Don't look at me like that. Yeh, I live off your garbage. I touch it every day. Examine it. Study it. Meditate on it. Your own personal garbage, the stuff you think isn't good enough for *your* life anymore. The parts of your life you try and make disappear into the category of non–worth, non–value, non–existence—just garbage. Then someone like me comes along and digs it all out...and reads it...wears it...eats it...gives it another chance in the world. Oh, yeh, you can tell a lot about a person by what they decide is garbage.

I know a lot about garbage. Garbage stinks. Garbage rots. Garbage ebbs and garbage flows. But garbage don't cry. And after I rescued that corned beef and was closing the lid on the dumpster, I heard a sound down inside it, deep down. Something weak...and faint...and...and pissed off.

I looked back in, and there was a bunch of flies buzzing like hell around one big black bag in the corner. I took my cane and poked it, and the sound came out of it again, this time louder...and more pissed off. I pulled the bag and ripped it open and inside...inside...stuffed in a Macy's shopping bag...and wrapped up in a couple towels...with an argyle sock jammed in its mouth...was a baby. Turning purple. Dying. And being *really* pissed off about the whole thing.

The cops came and took it away. But I gotta wonder: what kinda person hated a part of their life so bad, they threw this baby in the garbage? Just threw it out like yesterday's corned beef...for someone like me...someone like *me*...to give it another chance in the world.

Oh, yeh.

You can tell a lot about a person by what they decide is garbage.

Express Lane

(female)

Will you look at that, Marjorie? Some people. The nerve. I'm telling you. The sign says "Express Lane—8 Items Or Less". Am I wrong? Eight items. Not nine, not ten, not fifty–one–point–oh–fourteen, eight. You tell me—if that's eight items in her basket, I'm a Chiquita banana.

What? Maybe she can't read? Or maybe she can't count? So, I'm responsible to suffer for her bad schooling? Am I right? Am I wrong? She must have a lifetime supply of Hershey bars in that basket. Some people have no consideration. No decency. No respect for other people's human rights. Years from now when they talk about the downfall of American civilization? This is where it started, Marjorie: the Express Lane in Sugarman's Stop 'n' Save. Am I right? Am I wrong? She must have the entire frozen dinner section in there! You think that's a wig? I think it's a wig. Has to be. A woman her age...look at her come on to the bag boy.

Mygod, Marjorie, look, look, look...she's digging in the purse for, what—food stamps, no doubt. Government takes our hard–earned tax dollars, gives to lazy no–goodniks who get in a wrong checkout line and harass the honest hard–working citizen—oh god, no, worse—*coupons!* She's dragging out coupons by the handful. It's a blizzard of coupons. I cannot believe this! Cash only in the express lane, cash only, cash only! No coupons, no coupons, no coupons, no coupons!

The hussy, she's practically giving the bag boy a guided tour down the inside of her blouse. She's a menace, that one. Somebody oughta stop her. Now what? She's gonna show the bag boy her family photo album? Go on, marry the kid, honey; take him home and marry him; get him bar mitzvahed first, then marry him, just get outa the line, get outa the line, get outa the line!

Whew. Finally. Some people. The nerve. Am I right? Am I wrong? I don't know about you, Marjorie, but shopping is hell, whoops, there she goes, I gotta run. Hey, ma! Ma, wait up! What? I *would* be done already if you didn't bring half the supermarket into the express lane! So *give* the bag boy his tip and let go his necktie! He's too young for you, it'll never work out. *Maaaaa!*

Family Man

(male)

I can see you're a family man. That's nice. That's good. Family is good. Hey, nice tie, yeh.

I can always tell a family man. They got a certain look. Certain style. Certain way they hold themselves. They dress...well, they dress like you. Responsible. Satisfied. In control. Hey, nice shoes, yeh, comfy, too, I bet.

You got kids? Sure you do. Now *that's* responsibility. Teaching a kid right from wrong. It's tough I know, I know. I didn't get a good start in that department. *My* father didn't...take responsibility for that. So I had to find a way to get that responsibility into my life, you understand?

Is that shirt genuine silk? Really? Thought so. You look like a guy would wear genuine silk shirts. Like a guy would take *responsibility* to wear genuine silk shirts. Like a guy would know how really important it is to *take* that kind of responsibility. Cause that's what's dragging this world into the pits, you know that, I know you do. No one will take responsibility for nothing no more. Responsibility is, like, a dirty word or something, I don't know, people just don't have no use for it no more, it's terrible, it really is.

That's why we're alike, me and you. We're family men. With responsibility. Like the responsibility I got. For you. You did something unresponsible, my friend, I don't know what it was, but now—*(pulls a pistol from inside his coat)*—you got to take responsibility and set a good example for your kids.

Kneel down. C'mon, kneel. Kneel for me, okay? No, I can't, mister. No. I'm sorry. I cannot oblige me. I got my responsibility. You can understand that, can't you? Watch your knees there, you'll get your pants mushed, what are they gabardine? They're sharp.

C'mon, c'mon, don't cry. You can understand. You got a responsibility. You're a family man. *(cocks hammer, aims)*

So am I. *(fires...twice)*

Girl Talk

(female)

Hi, mom. It's Kimberley. Uh–huh, college is super. Yeh, oh, they're really rad, oh, the best ever. They're these super–cool sun-blockers that change color when your cholesterol level goes into overdrive—huh? Oh, my *classes*, I thought you said *glasses*. Oh, yeh, classes are okay. It's all that, you know, English and stuff where you have to write about books you have to read outside of class on your own free time, I mean, isn't that against the Constitution or something? I don't take history till sophomore year.

Anyway, I wanted to talk. Just you and me—like girl talk. Are you sitting down? Um, well, this guy I know, wait, let me start over, no, no, it's not what you think, um, well, this guy, what's his name? Ummmmm, I don't know. No, it's not what you think, mom, are you really sitting down? Okay, well, I was at this sorority rush annnnnnnd, I met this guuuuuuy, and he had this *incredible* tattoo on his, um, well, I didn't actually see it, I just *heard* about it, um, mom, it's *not* what you think, chill, mom, chill, mom, please? Okay?

Okay, well, one thing led to another, no wait, that's not what I—okay, we met this friend of his, and *his* name was Blade—I don't know, I guess it's his first name. Anyway, Blade drove me back to the dorm, just part–way cause his Harley ran out of gas right outside this bar on the edge of town, no, I don't know what town it was, but the bar was called The Doll House or something about toys, and anyway, we went inside to make a phone call and—what? Yes, I know I'm only eighteen, but, like, I guess the fishnet halter top I had on made me look older, wait, no that's not what I—okay, chill, mom, chill, mom, please! Anyway we go inside, and a bunch of Blade's friends just, like, happened to be there having a party cause they'd just got out on parole or some-thing, and so I had a few more little drinks, but it was okay cause Blade said they were only alcoholic lite, and next thing I know I'm up dancing on the stage, and everybody's clapping and shouting, so I kept dancing, and guys started throwing money onstage, though credit cards would've been better or maybe gift certificates from The Gap, but finally, it was time to go home and then some other guys jumped up and said they were from the police and this was, like, a bust, and everybody had to get down on the floor, except for me, cause I went out the back door with this one guy who is, like dean of the liberal arts school, and he said if I didn't say anything about him being there to his wife or the newspapers or the other deans, he would, like, give me a full scholarship all three years. Huh? College has *four* years? Now you tell me!

An Artist Like Me

(male)

What is this? I ordered mashed potatoes and gravy and I got the toxic waste from the Black Lagoon gushin' out here.

Hey. You. C'mere, babe. Closer. Listen to me...you're not a waitress. You know that. I know that. You just blew into town from down–state somewheres. Your boyfriend is back at the apartment layin' around watchin' soapies while you're pumpin' pasta and runnin' your tootsies to the nub. Do I got that right? Hey, he got you this far, and now it's up to *you* to make the next move. Cause you're not really a waitress. You know that. I know that. These schmucks here don't know that, that's their problem, they'll figure out if you give 'em a shovel and a toothpick.

C'mere, babe. Closer. Listen to me...I know you got plans. Me too. I got plans like you got plans, and you know what? I bet the plans I got are just like the plans you got. You're too good for this place, and you got talent. You're an artist. An ar–*tiste*. Like me. You know that. I know that, we're in agreement, we're soul mates, hey—what you need is somebody who can work with your talent. Somebody can see...The Big Picture. Somebody who's been...Down the Road. Somebody can take you...Right Where You Wanna Go.

C'mere, babe. Closer. Listen to me...I want you to succeed. I want you to be The Next Big Thing cause, babe, you are It. I'm lookin' at you, at that face, at that smile, at that beauty, at that essence, at that at that that *uunnhh* you got right there inside you, and I'm sayin', "Hey...I could work with this girl. I could make her happen in a very, very big way. I could make her every dream come true. I could give her what she's always wanted. Cause I know what that is. I know exactly what this girl has always wanted, and I am here, right here at *this* counter in front of *these* mashed potatoes for the sole purpose of giving her what *she* wants—and *needs*."

C'mere, babe. Closer. Listen to me...we gotta talk. Serious. About our future. You get off at one? Good. I'll be here. We can relax, have a drink, get some things out in the open. Cause you got talent. You're an ar–*tiste*. Like me.

Thanks for Calling

(male)

Good evening, Robinson residence. Yes, this is Danny Robinson, who is this? Murray? Murray who? Sorry, I don't— what? Murray? *Murray!* Yes! Murray, Murray, Murray, Murray, Murray! Yehhhhhh, Murray!

I'm sorry, I don't know any Murray K. Stephanopoulos, Junior—you must have the wrong number. What? Oh! *That* Murray K. Stephanopoulos, Junior! Well, why didn't you say so? Gosh, it's been, what, gosh, well, way too long! No, I was just kidding around, of course I knew who you were—only the best darn college roommate I ever had. Truly!

Me? Well, to tell you the truth, I, uh, I've had some ups and downs lately. Janis and I aren't, well, we're not doing so well. No, it's fine, Murray, really, it was just the pressure of—well, about nine months ago I lost my job at Amalgamated. Downsizing, you know; haven't worked since. Then there was the house. It burned down. Accident, of course, *somebody* left their curling iron on. The next week little Lisa fell off the back yard swing and broke her neck and—yes, total paralysis, no, it's okay, really, you can rent a good cheap iron lung for, oh, twelve hundred dollars a day. And about a month after that, the twins—Murray, you took biology, did you ever hear of a rare blood disorder called 'Lyptophenacorpulegia'? I know, it was a shock to us too, yes, both of them, just like that, very rare, very rare. And then the lawsuits—at the service Janis left the car motor running, and the gear slipped into reverse, and the crazy thing just ran by itself all through the entire cemetery for about an hour until it went off the cliff onto the trailer park below. Only a *few* bystanders, not more than a dozen, no, no, she's *fine*, she, uh, resides at Riverview now; yes, Riverview Asylum, doctors aren't optimistic.

So, Murray, how're things with you?

Well, I've tried to keep a perspective about it all. I tried religion. I tried drink. Then last month I had a sex–change operation. Call me Daniella, darling. Yes, still a redhead, but only my hairdresser knows for sure, heh–heh–heh. His name's Rene, do you want his number? No, well, it *has* been nice talking to you,

Murray; sorry you have to rush off. Anytime you want to get together and chat about old times—yes, thanks for calling. Bye–bye.

What? No, hon, just some jerk I used to know in college. Tell Lisa and the twins to come down now if they want a ride to the playground. The Bears game starts in a half hour, and I gotta go back to the office and finish up the McAllister proposal tonight.

Jeez! Some people will say *anything* to sell you insurance.

Door to Door

(female)

Good morning, sir, how are you today? Is the lady of the house at home? No? Well, I'm sure you'll be equally excited to hear about our newest product, the Acme Deluxe Boutique Lemonfresh Foot Refresher Kit, perfect for spa, bath or boudoir and only seven–ninety–nine, local sales tax and shipping–slash–delivery charges not included. May I demonstrate this amazing specialty gift item and holiday stocking stuffer for you, sir? It takes only three minutes, and a lifetime of ablutorial pleasure and unadulterated hygienic elegance can be yours for mere pennies a day.

Why, thank you. What a lovely home! Oh, I cannot tell you how utterly tasteful and healing this is. May I sit? Thank you. Now, if you wouldn't mind removing your shoe and sock—left or right, either one. There. My, what an interesting foot! Hmmm. Oh, nothing. I was just thinking that the last time I saw a foot with *this* particular contour...well, it's nothing to worry about. Not *really.* Of course, nearly every human illness is rooted in the feet. You didn't know that? Why, it's a well–documented—oh my goodness—do you see this bump here? Hmmmm. Sir, are you by any chance presently wrestling with dilemma in your marital sphere? Hmmmm. I see. A bump here by the instep represents fear of the future and of not being willing to take a forward step in your emotional life. Now, while we rub in this gentle, soothing massage lotion, you can repeat this simple affirmation—take my a hand and chant with me— "I move onward in my life with ecstasy and ease; I do not stumble nor yield to the bitter burning bunions of fear and hyper–disharmony." Oh, that is very good, sir, very, very good. Yes, let it out, let it all out. Let the rage flow, let the anger come, ohyes, ohyes, oh let the healing come, oh doesn't that feel good? Release the guilt, release the tension, release the persecuting attitudes...here, smell this? This is a dab of our polyglycerine soap, finely scented with the ultimate in masculine fragrance, and if we apply it right...here...ooooh, doesn't that tingle? Well, it's supposed to, and it represents the very deep criticism you have of your inner child, oh come on, sir, wipe away those lumps of undissolved anger, keep chanting, keep chanting, there is nothing to be ashamed of. Now, here is our patented micro–mini–massager, let me plug it in, batteries not included, and—*ooooh!*—doesn't that just vibrate you down to your tippy–tippy–tippy–toes? Mmmm, ohyes, ohyes, we accept all major credit cards, ohyes, ohyes, mmmm, please add in a counseling gratuity of fifteen per cent, ohyes, and we'll send you a free video C.O.D. for only thirty–nine–ninety–nine entitled *Cosmic Footprints: Birkenstocks of the Creator Gods*, ohyes, ohyes, ohyes, ohyes!

Something To Do

(male)

It was just, like, something to do.

Kids today don't have enough to do. It's a generation thing. Like, our parents, it's *their* fault. When we're little they put us in front of the TV for hours at a time, and then they get spiffed because now we don't like to read books. When we're older they leave us at the mall for hours at a time, and if we, like, shoplift or something or spray some paint on some dumb sign, it's, like, supposed to be our fault? We're, like, master criminals? It was just, like, something to do.

I mean, it's a generation thing. Our parent's generation invented the atomic bomb and were always starting wars all over the world, and, like, bazillions of people died, and there are still millions and millions of really poor people everywhere, and they treat us like it's our fault. I mean, I was at Jason's house last week. We'd both cut school and his parents were at work and we wanted to go to the mall but we didn't have any money. So he said we should check out his stepdad's closet and maybe we'd find some. So, I said, "Rad, dude!", and we started looking, and Jason opened this box, and it had a gun in it, like a nine millimeter or something. "Cool!" I said. "Totally awesome!" And Jason said, "Hey, man, is this the first real gun you ever saw?" And I said, "Hell, no!" Though, actually it was, but when I picked it up and closed my fingers around the grip, it felt just like a part of my hand. It felt really cool. Smooth and cool and good. Slim and solid. Like a missing part of my hand. Like, this is weird maybe—but I wanted to take it to bed with me and, like, rub my stiffie on it, it felt that good.

Then Jason said we should go to the mall and show it to the kids for money, and so we did. Then this old guy bumped into Freddie, just some dumbass old bald guy like my father's age, and Jason said, "Hey, dorkface," to the guy. "Watch where you're going, buttwad!" And the guy turned and said something to Jason, and Jason threw his Pepsi in the guy's face, and the guy dropped his packages and started to grab at Jason, and Jason said, "Get him off me! He's killing me! Get him off!, and so I took the gun and pointed it at the guy, and the gun, like...it just went off...in the guy's face...as he was looking at me...his face just...like, blew up...and blood gushed everywhere and skin and and and and...and everybody just stood there and watched the guy lay on the ground, and I thought, "This is, like, a movie; this is not real," but the gun was still in my hand, and I never thought it was loaded or anything. I mean, it wasn't really my fault. I'm, like, an evil terrorist or something?

I mean, it was just, like, something to do.

Let Jesus Be Your Pit Stop in the Final Race to Heaven

(male)

Now, friends, though you might think you're on the highway to salvation, if you just sit there in the moral middle of the road, that sweet heavenly chariot's gonna run you right over! Life is not a limo ride, pilgrims, and nobody ever got to meet Jesus by bumming rides on another person's running board.

In fact, I was once a lot like all of you—a splendid, splendid sinner. I was a hot rod racer, a genuine thrill chaser, speedin' my life away on a quarter–mile strip. Fast cars and faster women—and, oh Lord yes, too much whiskey—made me feel I was gonna lose my grip. I'd run on every dirt track from Idaho to Tennessee; had diesel in my veins, rubber in my brain and not a friend in the world for me. I was headed for a spinout—I'd just about lost my nerve—when a Voice rang out above me as I rounded Dead Man's Curve.

It said, "Let Jesus be your pit stop in the final race to heaven; He'll keep your wheels a–turnin' night and day. Let His scriptures be your road signs and His angels be your pit crew, makin' sure your soul don't go astray."

Now when you're in the fast lane, but you got no chance of winnin', take a little time to gas up with the Lord. Just pull alongside Jesus and let Him check you over and get you ready for your just reward. His oil is the finest, made from His precious blood; his parts will last forever, they saved Noah from the flood. Don't let backsliders tempt you with a cheaper brand; just follow His directions, and you'll reach the Promised Land.

Cause He's the Leader of the Pack with the key to the highway; don't nobody know life's route like Him. He'll guide you through the chuckholes and keep your headlights shinin' even when the road looks dark and grim. He'll never let you blow out; He'll never let you crash. He'll always steer you straight ahead when you keep Him on your dash. And when you take the white flag and you got one lap to go; He'll be waitin' with St. Peter wavin' you right on home.

So, let Jesus be your pit stop in the final race to heaven; He'll keep your wheels a–turnin' night and day. Let His scriptures be your road signs and His angels be your pit crew, makin' sure your soul don't go astray. I said, makin' sure your soul don't go astray. Whoa now, thank you, Jesus, thank you, Jesus, thank you, thank you, Jesus!

Now, church, if you'll kindly pass the collection basket among you; ain't nobody ever said the highway to heaven wasn't a toll road.

Help 'em Forget

(female)

I can understand you tryin' to put on fancy airs and get over on a new chippie. That's good for my business. For every woman come in here sniffin' round after you, there's twenty men trailin' in behind sniffin' after her! But why you tryin' to impress all these high–tone people? They ain't gonna let you be nothin' 'cept what you already are. You just wastin' your time, and, sugar, *your* time is *my* time.

See this? Yeh, all these empty tables and chairs. Well, they mine. I own 'em. Every last one of 'em. And my business is to fill 'em up—every night—with hard–workin' men and women wanna drink lotsa liquor, drink it hard and drink it fast, so they can forget what a stink–ass world it is where they just come from. Now, *your* music supposed to help 'em forget. Your music ain't supposed to educate 'em, or give 'em Jesus or stir 'em up and get 'em marchin' outa here to go vote for no damn politicians gonna give us no damn new deal same as the old deal!

Your music supposed to help 'em *forget*. And, sugar, that's somethin' you better always remember.

Love Me Two Times

(male)

At the Boogie Rock Club in Hue City, all the girls had American Top Forty names. There was White Rabbit. Mustang Sally. Inna Gadda Da Vida. Lucy in the Sky with Diamonds. Jennifer Juniper. Da Doo Ron Ron. Sugar Pie Honeybunch. The madam figured it made the boys feel more at home. And she was right.

The most popular with our unit was Love Me Two Times. Didn't speak much English. Didn't have to really. Had what you call a winning personality. She laughed a lot and sang "Love me two times, baby, love me twice today; love me two times, babe, cause I'm goin' away" over and over and over again, just laughing and singing and laughing and singing.

One night just before we were headed in country with a convoy to Can Tho, me and a new guy from Philly named Bergman went to the Boogie Rock. Bergman was just a kid, eighteen, nineteen thereabouts. Short with a funny little round face and glasses and a nose that twitched up and down when he talked. Had a little rabbity way of walking, kinda hoppy like. Like Bugs Bunny on acid.

This night all the girls were occupied. Except for Love Me Two Times. So me and Bergman, we flipped for her. And he won. I think he was a damn virgin, tell you the truth.

"Be gentle with him," I says to Love Me Two Times, laughing. And she laughs back, and I go downstairs to the bar to wait my turn. Not seeing, of course, Love Me Two Times slip out the back. After having took a satchel charge from her panties and put it under the bed. And two minutes later, Bergman didn't have no arms or no legs. Just a head...a trunk...and four red stumps.

Took him four damn days to die. Four damn days. Just a kid...eighteen, nineteen thereabouts.

I had to write a letter to his folks saying he died a good marine.

But no way could I tell them he died a damn virgin.

Flashbacks Burn

(male)

    Lowell George croons "I will be your Dixie chicken, if you'll be my Tennessee lamb" on the all–nite oldies station, as I fluff a pillow next to my wife and watch tears suddenly spurt from her crumpling face when she leafs through a Canadian literary magazine she picked up after Twelve Step this afternoon at a yard sale because of the neo–Warhol cover and learns on page nine that her college roommate was killed last year for three dollars in a Chicago parking garage and the man who wrote the poem about it still dreams of her and my wife dancing together at the Stones show after Kent State, the twenty–fifth anniversary of which is being marked by a special commemorative designer flatware set available for only nineteen–ninety–nine on the Good Karma Home Shopping Channel bringing you on–the–spot coverage of next month's Strawberry Alarm Clock reunion tour of North Dakota, and right then all I could do was pull the covers over my head and wish every goddam radio and teevee in the world would just blow a fuse and shut up for good, cause flashbacks burn baby burn baby burn.

I Once Was Scared of the Dark

(female/male)

I once was scared of the dark. Just about a year ago. When I was five. I was scared cause when I went to sleep, I had bad dreams. So I didn't want to go to sleep, and I didn't want to be anywhere in the dark. Alone. Or I would cry. And sometimes throw up.

The worst bad dream I had was that I was in a playground. Playing. With my friends all around and then all of a sudden, they weren't there, and I was alone. And it all of a sudden got real dark. And then a man dressed up like candy cane would chase me. And I would cry, because it was dark, and I was alone. And I had this dream lots of nights.

My mom said it was just a bad dream, but just because that's true doesn't mean she is psychic. Nobody is psychic, because if they were, they could take over the world. But nobody is psychic, and I am glad because they could come over to my house and take over my house. But then that wouldn't matter, cause I would just go to the toy store and get a toy rifle and make it look like a real one, and I could scare them away just like that. Did you know I once got my right arm shut in the trunk of my dad's car? And I fell down off the slide and cut my head open and that was on October 10, which was very close to my birthday. And that's when I climbed the tree in back of the garage where I used to think the candy cane man lived.

Now, isn't that a coincidence?

Then this one night I looked at the garage and saw the candy cane man dancing on top of it. And he came closer, and he whispered my name real quiet cause he didn't want anyone to hear, and I knew this time he was going to kill me, and I got scared, and I yelled for my mom. "Mom! Mommmm! Help me, please, the candy cane man is coming to get me! Look out there, the candy cane man is there! He's coming to get us! Help me, *pleaaaassssssssse! Mommmmmmmm!*"

And then I woke up, cause I had only been dreaming, but I

was crying. And my mom came, and you know what she did? She took a kleenex and waved it all over my bed. And then she went to my window and opened it up and waved the kleenex around. I said, "Mom, are you wacko?", and she said she was pushing all the bad dreams out the window, and they would never come back. And she flushed the kleenex down the potty and then kissed me good night, and I went to sleep.

And that's how come I'm not scared of the dark anymore. Cause I know now that for the rest of my life, even when I get real old, like maybe nineteen or twenty, all I have to do to make bad people go away and not hurt me is take a kleenex and flush them down the potty.

Advice Lady

(female)

If you ask me, she should dump the putz. I mean, he's done nothing for her, and she's got her own life to live, you know what I mean? And what he did behind her back with those scrawny little shiksas on the beach? If you ask me, he's history, finito, end of story, cease and desist, kaputsky, nada, nyet, zippo, zilch—ohmygod, Erica, don't get me started on the Royal Family again! The world is such a heartless place!

Look at those two over there. On the bench in front of Seidelman's. What is he doing with her pantyhose? What, is he painting her knees, what? What, what is he doing to her? I am *not* a busybody, Erica! This is a public spot, I am a public person, and painting graffiti on a woman's pantyhose on the sidewalk is a public act! This *is* my business! For all you know he could be a masher. Or one of those, what do you call them, fetshuganists?

If you ask me, he's not bad–looking. Looks like he's giving her a medical examination. Do you think he's a doctor or what? Maybe I should tell him about my Natalie. She won't marry until she finds Mr. Right, and that could be the next millennium. I told her, I said, "Natalie, if you ask me, but you won't because I'm only your mother, if you ask me, you're too choosy, and in this world you're never going to find Mr. Right. Mr. Okay, Mr. Not–So–Bad, Mr. Could–Be–Worse—maybe. That is if some low–life like Glenda Ruble doesn't sink her hooks into him first and make shredded wheat out of him." That one is a man–killer, Erica! Pure venom dripping from her dentures. But, like I told my Natalie, people ask me for advice all the time, and what's the point of giving it? Nobody listens? Nobody listens to a thing I say! Why do you think that is, Erica? Erica? Erica, wake up. Wake up and have a blintz. Ohmygod, what is he doing to her ankle? If you ask me, those two are breaking some kind of law. They're having entirely too much fun.

Disciple of the Demitasse

(female)

Thank you, Renaldo. Yes, send a waiter over in a few minutes, and we'll order appetizers. Charming, isn't he? He looks even better after a double mocha expresso with a twist of ginseng and dash of Courvoisier. Yes, darling, coffee has become my performance art. Isn't it utterly indecorous?

I mean, really, darling, what do you want me to do with my time? Take up the harmonica? Join a birdwatching club? Shop till I drop? Collect expensive trinkets and meaningless baubles? Drink cheap white wine and drive aimlessly around town all day seeking naive but firmly–muscled young boys for an evening's jaded debauchery? Well, I've done all that, and it didn't make me happy. Not like coffee. Coffee is my one true rapture.

Nonsense! Coffee doesn't affect the nervous system at all. That's a hideous fabrication of the laxative industry. Ooops, sorry! They fill these cream containers to excess, don't worry, it'll bleach out. Waiter! Bring a towel, please! What? On an average day I drink maybe eight cups. An unaverage day? Maybe thirty–five or forty. But, you must understand, I am a *connoisseur.* A savant of the noble bean. A dedicated disciple of the demitasse. Coffee isn't a filthy habit like cigarettes or polo players; it's an art form. The final aesthetic frontier. A sublime act of veneration to Mother Nature in her purest aromatic form. Coffee is gentle. Coffee is forgiving. Coffee is compassionate. And I am dedicating my life to mastering its nuances, its subtleties, its sybaritic, seductive intimacies, its elusive, hidden secrets portending ageless wisdom of the Earth.

Are you feeling well, darling? You haven't said a word since we sat down. Here, have some coffee. There you go. The things that's crucial to remember about coffee is—ooops! Sorry, darling, my fault again, how clumsy of me. Waiter! Bring a towel, please! Yes, *another* towel. There's been *another* accident. Yes, I believe it *is* customary to receive one towel per accident. Do you have to file a police report before you bring it here? My apologies, darling, it is *so* hard to get good help these days—ooops! Will you get *out* of the way? I'm trying to do your job and clean up this mess! Of all the insolent—Renaldo! Renaldo! Come here at once! Have some of my coffee, darling, yours seems to keep getting spilled, no, it's not too strong, you'll love it—Renaldo! Ooops! My goodness, darling, I, this table is as crooked as a ram's horn! It's practically ready to collapse! Why is the table shaking? Renaldo! Oops! I am *so* sorry, darling—did you feel that? It's an earthquake! My god, look at the table shake! When did they start having earthquakes in Des Moines? Renaldo!

Music of Your Life*

(male)

When I was a kid I had a little cheap transistor radio stuck in my ear all day—everywhere I went and at night under the covers. I could tune out the uptight little farmtown world I was in and tune in the big groovy, funkytown world I knew was waiting just beyond. Not a minute didn't go by without some song telling my whole world like it was and like it oughta be. *Blame it on the Bossa Nova*, it's the dance of love. Yeh, he's the *Leader of the Pack*. *Earth Angel,* earth angel, whoa–oh–oh–oh, please be mine. *Return to Sender,* address unknown. She's my little *Four–Oh–Nine,* Four–Oh–Nine, Four–Oh–Nine. Everybody's gone surfin', *Surfin' U.S.A. He's So Fine,* oo–lang, oo–lang. *Hit the Road, Jack* and don't you come back no more no more. Duke, Duke, Duke, *Duke of Earl*, Earl, Earl. Come on, baby, do–ooo *The Locomotion* with me. *Mister Bass Man*, you set the music thumping with a ba–ba–ba, ba–ba–ba and a ba–ba dit–dit dingaling dit–dit.

Damn, that was music! Then that Beatle thing happened and all them English groups come over and then Motown and the acid stuff come out. Doors and Canned Heat and Hendrix and Cream, and we really begun to rock like it would never stop.

Summer of '71 I was nineteen hitching from Toledo more or less to New York after I quit that dishwashing job at the Ponderosa. I'd just seen the MC5 and Ted Nugent in Detroit and they kicked ass lemme tell you, talked all about the revolution right around the corner and the new shape of things to come. I was ready!

Round midnight I had a ride on the New York Thruway with a Tennessee trucker and his amphetamine collection somewhere near Utica or Syracuse, and Reverend Ike was on the radio screaming and hollering with the spirit of Jesus Christ the Sears Siding Salesman loud enough to wake the dead and scare the come right outa the living.

Then the news come on, and they said something about the draft lottery numbers, and the trucker he pulled out a Marlboro and lit up. "When's your birthday, son?" he asked me, and I told him, and he said he guessed I oughta feel lucky cause I just won the big prize at Mr. Nixon's tea party. "Your birthday's Number One, kid," he said and gave me a swig of his Colt .45 just as the news ended and the music come back on with Credence—*Don't go out tonight, it's bound to take your life...There's a bad moon on the rise*—and that's how I knew I was going to Nam.

Knew I was leaving Nam when I heard *Billy, Don't Be a Hero*, and I sat up on the operating table looking down at the inside of my left thigh.

---

*song titles and lyrics in italics should be sung

Smith and Kraus *Books For Actors*
THE MONOLOGUE SERIES
> The Best Men's / Women's Stage Monologues of 1994
> The Best Men's / Women's Stage Monologues of 1993
> The Best Men's / Women's Stage Monologues of 1992
> The Best Men's / Women's Stage Monologues of 1991
> The Best Men's / Women's Stage Monologues of 1990
> One Hundred Men's / Women's Stage Monologues from the 1980's
> 2 Minutes and Under: Character Monologues for Actors
> Street Talk: Character Monologues for Actors
> Uptown: Character Monologues for Actors
> Monologues from Contemporary Literature: Volume I
> Monologues from Classic Plays
> 100 Great Monologues from the Renaissance Theatre
> 100 Great Monologues from the Neo-Classical Theatre
> 100 Great Monologues from the 19th C. Romantic and Realistic Theatres

FESTIVAL MONOLOGUE SERIES
> The Great Monologues from the Humana Festival
> The Great Monologues from the EST Marathon
> The Great Monologues from the Women's Project
> The Great Monologues from the Mark Taper Forum

YOUNG ACTORS SERIES
> Great Scenes and Monologues for Children
> New Plays from A.C.T.'s Young Conservatory
> Great Scenes for Young Actors from the Stage
> Great Monologues for Young Actors
> Multicultural Monologues for Young Actors
> Multicultural Scenes for Young Actors

SCENE STUDY SERIES
> Scenes From Classic Plays 468 B.C. to 1960 A.D.
> The Best Stage Scenes of 1993
> The Best Stage Scenes of 1992
> The Best Stage Scenes for Men / Women from the 1980's

CONTEMPORARY PLAYWRIGHTS SERIES
> Romulus Linney: 17 Short Plays
> Eric Overmyer: Collected Plays
> Lanford Wilson: 21 Short Plays
> William Mastrosimone: Collected Plays
> Horton Foote: 4 New Plays
> Israel Horovitz: 16 Short Plays
> Terrence McNally: 15 Short Plays
> Humana Festival '93: The Complete Plays
> Humana Festival '94: The Complete Plays
> Women Playwrights: The Best Plays of 1992
> Women Playwrights: The Best Plays of 1993

GREAT TRANSLATION FOR ACTORS SERIES
> The Wood Demon by Anton Chekhov

CAREER DEVELOPMENT SERIES
> The Camera Smart Actor
> The Sanford Meisner Approach
> The Actor's Chekhov
> Kiss and Tell: Restoration Scenes, Monologues, & History
> Cold Readings: Some Do's and Don'ts for Actors at Auditions

If you require pre-publication information about upcoming Smith and Kraus books, you may receive our semi-annual catalogue, free of charge, by sending your name and address to *Smith and Kraus Catalogue, P.O. Box 127, One Main Street, Lyme, NH 03768. Or call us at (800) 895-4331, fax (603) 795-4427.*